Entrepreneur-ing –

How to Use Entrepreneurial

Skills to Launch Your Own

Business or to be the Boss of

Your Career

Written by Lisa Vento Nielsen, MBA, PMP

Lisa Vento Nielsen is a business executive, educator and entrepreneur. She has over 13 years' experience in Corporate America and Higher Education. With her work in Corporate America, she has extensive hiring and resume experience. As an adjunct professor at local NYC colleges, her insight into what colleges want and how to present yourself is extremely valuable for your next step.

Lisa has a BS degree in Marketing and a MBA in International Finance, both from St John's University. Her MBA is from the Rome, Italy campus of St John's University, where she learned how to speak Italian. Upon returning to the United States, she began her career in the financial services and publishing industries. She excelled at Project Management and is a certified Project Management Professional since 2004 with PMI.

She left Corporate America to focus on teaching and entrepreneurial pursuits. Lisa began teaching at the University level in 2003 and learned she has a passion and a knack for teaching complex topics with a mix of real world and academic expertise.

Lisa has run her own businesses over the years as a consultant preparing business plans, editing and improving resumes and helping businesses, professionals and students take their next step.

Dedicated to: My children, Sofia and Christopher Nielsen

Entrepreneur-Ing How to Use Entrepreneurial Skills to Launch Your Own Business or to be the Boss of Your Career

Table of Contents:

Introduction:

Too many people are passive in terms of their goals and plans. I do not say this to be confrontational or mean – from my decade plus experiences as an educator, executive and entrepreneur, I have seen first-hand how often people shy away from pushing for the big opportunities.

This book is for you – those of you who did not negotiate their job offers, those of you who downplay your skills and talents – you need me to help you identify your strengths and rock them out like only you can. As I tell my clients, there is only one you (I tell my children that, too) – it is true.

You are the only one who can do the things you can. I believe everyone can benefit from this book on how to use entrepreneur-ing to launch a business or rock your career. If you are interested in one day being your own boss and running your own company, this book is for you. If you are interested in being the boss of your career *today* this book is for you. You do not need to be your own company to be a boss. You just need to identify how to rock out on your career as if you are CEO of yourself.

The post that germinated this idea from LinkedIn that I wrote is here:

"**Entrepreneurial career planning** I have found myself repeating the same idea around how important it is to manage your career as if it were your own business that I thought it would make sense to expand upon it more here on Pulse and also on my Blog.

When you own your own business you are the only one responsible for your success and your failure. Sometimes when you work for a big company, you give up that "hunger" or that feeling of being in "control". If we manage our careers like a business we can be more proactive about our path our skills and thus lead to a great level of success. And while doing this, we will, by default, be ahead of the competition.

How to do this is to keep in mind what it means to be entrepreneurial. I have had over 10 years of experience as an entrepreneur. I launched my own business called Business Tools 2 Go in 2002; this was before technology existed as it does now (for more see Technology for Small Business).

In 2005, my husband and I owned our own small store on Staten Island; I was the business leader, he was the product guy as what we bought and sold was in his area of expertise. Of course, as you know, in 2012, I began working on what is now The Next Step.

I have learned, I have failed and I have taught along the way. I have taught a few students and clients along the way how to become entrepreneurs and have mentored some former students to work at getting their ideas patented. As we know, I am the #profwhomakesyoupresent and therefore always make my students give presentations (yes, I am one of those professors). Some of the ideas that the students have come up with in terms of starting their own business ventures have been awesome and amazing. A lot of these skills and tools has also been used by my clients in growing and expanding their careers.

In being an entrepreneur, you stay "hungry" - you are always thinking and planning the next step of your "venture". Why shouldn't you consider yourself to be a venture? For example, ask yourself what education or skill sets do you need to get to where you want to be in your career? Do you know where you want to be in your career? As a small business owner a few times over, I know how important it is to have a short, medium and long term plan for my business. I also applied those principles to my careers in Corporate America and Higher Ed (and now in education grades K-12).

Some of my lessons that I can teach you in terms of using entrepreneurial skills to build out your career are here:

- **Stay focused on your end goal** – do a check every 3-6 months about what your goal(s) are – do you want to be promoted to a management position at your current company? Or do you want to leave your current company and move on someplace else? Is your dream to be in another industry or field? Do you have a plan to achieve that? Some of my clients have spent a decade or more in an industry and are ready to move on and try something new – we have to have a plan for that and learning and courses plugged in to expand their horizons and to show the new industry they are ready to hit the ground running with new skills that are not inherent in said industry.

- **Learning** – this is so important – consider you and your career as being continually challenged with new classes that you MUST take – some of those classes come in the form of new books to read, new skills to learn, seminars to take and just continually being interested and connected into what you want to "grow" in to. By continuing to learn, you will continue to grow and get more and more out of yourself and your career.

- **Work on the soft skills as well as the hard skills**. Learn things like six sigma and achieve licenses as a Project Management Professional but also do not neglect the soft skills such as *public speaking* (of course) – consider joining a Toastmasters Organization if your company has one or there is one nearby. This is a great way to work on this skill set in a safe environment and it will help you build out your career in more ways than you can know. I will be writing a new post with video on some public speaking hacks and more this week so stay tuned for that.

- **Stay informed** - keep informed of the news and trends in your industry and/or the industry you want to join – do not trust that your company will keep you up to date on what is going on – be informed and able to discuss major and minor developments in your world. Be ready with that elevator pitch – imagine if you and the CEO are in the elevator together –what would you talk about have some industry or other ideas at the ready to discuss with him or her. And even if it is not the CEO but your department head or someone else farther up the chain than you, how can you impress them to help you build out your career. This is the way entrepreneurs think about every interaction – how can I impress people to think of me, to recommend me to consider hiring me for what I can do for them. Having this mindset as an employee can set you apart from the others.

What do you think of my lessons for managing your career as if it was your own business? Do you try to do these things already? Has it worked for you? Will you try these lessons out in 2016 and let me know how it works for you? Happy Hunting!"

This book is not for the faint of heart – I am a "do-er" more so than a teacher and I will be including real "work" for you to execute on to get you to be the best you can be in any field but particularly the field of YOU. You need to begin to think of yourself as your own industry and make plans accordingly. This book is applicable for both career and entrepreneurship – if you apply these principles to your career, you might find yourself launching your own business on the side, too.

There will be another installment book for this one on the launching process of a small business; this book will get your ready to launch your own business and maybe while you are also focusing on applying these skills to your regular career, too. So keep an eye out for updates for the next installment of this Entrepreneur-ing Series.

For every one client I have helped and for every 1,000 people who have read and learned from my blog on a weekly basis, I knew there was more I could do to share my message about being proactive and entrepreneurial in your career and your life.

So many people dream of being a small business owner, so many people are not ready to retire but find themselves forced to stop working because of corporate rules once they hit a certain age. Also much has been written and reported about trying to find a job in your late 40's and 50's. There is an issue across the board of maintaining and growing your career in the way you want it to be created. This can be alleviated by understanding and applying these steps to your career.

The most important thing I espouse and believe is that you must keep learning. The only way to succeed and build your career from A to Z is to learn – reading this book is one great big step forward in your learning process. I think that by spending this time with me in this book and reading my words and lessons is the equivalent of having one on one sessions with a top level career coach and it can be done on your own time.

I have been a professor since 2003 and a Project Management Professional since 2004; therefore, this book is the crossroads of two very important fields that can lead to the most actionable results. I have broken this book up like the course structure I follow as a professor with inclusions of project management skills and know-how for you to execute on these lessons. There will also be an online component with videos available once this book is done.

There are 12 chapters in this book; much like there are 12 weeks in a course at any university. Many chapters end with "homework" and deliverables for you to execute on for project based learning.

I wish you luck and happy hunting! Thank you for learning with me.

Chapter 1:

Learning Plan

What does Entrepreneur-Ing Mean?

This word means so many things. What it means to you is that you are in the right place to do some self-directed learning from an expert on applying skills and traits of entrepreneurship to either your career or your business.

For those of you focused on building your own business, this book is the blueprint for you to follow to execute on your idea.

For those of you focused on building your career like a boss, this book is the blueprint for you to follow to learn how to make yourself the project of your life.

I was considering doing a choose your own adventure type book for this to provide a one way path for entrepreneur-ing your business and entrepreneur-ing your career but I feel it is best to teach you both sides of the coin in terms of this phenomenon. If you can master entrepreneurship for your business, you will have the tools necessary for when / if you need a steady income and to build out a career in corporate

America. For those of you brave enough to learn how to be entrepreneurial in your career, the potential for opening up your own business is definitely something that will happen organically for you.

Why be an entrepreneur and create your own business:

For many subsets of the population, particularly women and minorities, the focus is on building value in your lives through your own businesses. The rates of entrepreneurship has been going through the roof.

For many people who are raising young children, having flexibility is key to the career path. I will not tell you being an entrepreneur is "easier" but you can work around your children's schedules a little more easily than at any established company.

If you have a passion or an idea, you need to learn how to nurture it and grow it. My unique advice will help you to focus on this venture as a part-time prospect at first – you can follow my steps and lessons while working full time or part time on the side or you can commit yourself to this system / learnings full time. In any way you slice or chunk it, your time will be best spent reading and learning from me in this book.

Why be an entrepreneur in your corporate career:

No one will look out for your growth and career as well as you can. You need to be proactive and focused in order to truly unlock your career potential. You can be anything you apply yourself to be if you can continue learning.

A big part of this book will teach you to have the drive and ability to continue learning at your speed and at your level. Not everyone will be an "A" student and not everyone should be – the goal is just to be a student period in any way shape of form to help continue to grow and learn on a daily basis. So much is changing in the field of careers and business with technology being poised to take over many jobs by 2020 that are now primarily held by women but can affect any gender. Your fields of customer service, banking, administrative assistants and more can be impacted by these leaps and bounds of technology and AI that can take away these roles.

This book breaks down the steps to be an entrepreneur with lessons on applying it to your career or your own venture (and many of you can do both sides of these lessons and win / win on every aspect of your lives).

I am your professor on this journey and we will be using my Web site and social media to learn from each other. I am a passionate teacher and have created and launched various curriculum to teach many different people many different things. I know there is no ONE way to learn – there are many ways to learn and that is why I am structuring this book with a feedback loop. Yes, a feedback loop. I want to build a relationship with each person that reads this book as a mentor to them – or as their own personal professor.

My lessons will focus on how to identify your skills to go from zero to launch. For the next step in your small business launch, there will be another installment in this series all about executing on the business plan and more.

This EBook and my others in draft are an interactive project that you can use my website to help build out and submit your video feedback to me for an interactive journey. You can also use my social media to discuss with me using tag #entrepreneur-ing.

This might be the first "ebook" of its kind that comes with its own professor. I am passionate about sharing this knowledge and in helping as many people as possible to unlock the careers they are destined to have. You can have a career as an entrepreneur or improve your career in corporate America (or insert any country, really) with me. I have experience as being an executive, educator and entrepreneur since 1999. I have lived and worked in other countries for various amounts of time and my focus on project management, teaching and learning means this book will walk you through your path unlike any other.

In Chapter 2, we will identify and expand on your skill sets for going from zero to launch in business and career. In Chapter 3 we will identify learning plans and paths to expand on said skills and how to achieve the new skills needed to rock out your career / business. Chapter 4 is about drafting the plan – just the mission statement; how to really dream it into action – by writing it down, you will make it real. This is where I will be making you respond to me; I will be waiting to hear and read your responses to this chapter.

Chapter 5 is all about building your brand and again this is where you will be following up with me and showing me your media brand and making me impressed with how you take it to the next level.

Chapter 6 is about writing your plan and includes templates and other resources for hitting it out of the ballpark with your communication skills. Chapter 7 discusses different ways to build your connections via networking, mentoring and more. Chapter 8 is about managing success and giving back, which is so important. I think all entrepreneur-ing people will be best served by giving back and doing it as soon as possible. I should move this chapter up higher because it is so important and maybe in future versions of this book I will move it up. Before I even was officially off the ground, I was considering ways to give back and my College Readiness Seminar and community outreach programs were launched before I even had my business "open".

Chapter 9 goes into the feedback loop.

This journey maybe has begun for you because you know deep down you can do more in your career. Or maybe it has begun because you have some blank spaces on your resume that you need to fill in and figure out how to make more meaning possible for your career and more. I have a lot to say about blank spaces and managing career and life transitions.

When you are faced with a blank space because of illness, child care or parental care or even due to self-care, you really need to look at that as being possibility and not liability. What can you do to manage through that time?

A big way to manage through that time is to identify skill sets you have that you can use in other ways that do not involve taking away from your current number one priority (the reason you have a blank space to begin with); or maybe you have blank spaces through no fault of your own but the economy has been unkind to you and you have yet to find your footing in corporate.

You can use this book to identify ways to set yourself apart from the competition by entrepreneur-ing your career. Not every entrepreneur is successful but we all have the grit and abilities to keep trying and putting ourselves out there very much like any job seeker has to do today. But the average job seeker will be shy or timid about opportunities and maybe will not put themselves out there as much as someone who is entrepreneur-ing will do and that is the difference between closing the sale, getting the offer and being able to manage your career like a boss.

That is where this book and its lessons come in to help you make the motions and move forward in a way to truly succeed.

I am so happy to take this journey with you and to build our relationship as more than just a book and an author but as your personalized professor / consultant on the road to entrepreneur-ing.

Something I have done as a professor since day one is to encourage my students to think outside of the box and I look forward to doing that with you – my mix of real-world advice with real actionable lessons and take away is what will set this book apart from any other how-to, business or other learning book you have read. I cannot wait to being this journey with you! You can learn so much and expand so much on your skills and abilities just by reading and acting on these lessons. Even if you only do a chapter at any time, you are heads above the competition that do not have this plan in hand to make their career/business stand out.

Happy entrepreneur-ing and running your career and business like a boss.

Chapter 2:

Identify your skills

What can you do to go from zero to launch in your business / career?

What do you want to do with your life? Remember when you were an undergrad (author's note: maybe you still are; welcome to my younger readers, you are in the right place because if you cannot have me as a real – life professor, having this book is the next best thing)? You have the whole world ahead of you and many different options depending on when you graduated.

If you graduated in the 1990's like I did, there was a bit of an economic contraction going on and jobs might have been tricky to find if you did not major in the right field. I had many super talented friends who could only find jobs in retail, in part because their majors maybe did not move them into job interviews. If you graduated in the 2000's you were ok unless you graduated in 2006-2009, in which case you got out of college and university in the midst of the financial crisis.

It used to be that you found a career and you were set once you got your foot in the door, you could work your way up and more. So many things have changed so rapidly such as technology, offshoring, outsourcing and more – I remember giving my students the reading assignments of "The World is Flat" and discussing it in each class when it was published.

Everyone would be shocked; meanwhile I had seen these things happen across the board in my career in Corporate America – roles were disappearing and people were being downgraded to not having real career options anymore. I had been entrepreneurial in nature since 2002; and have identified and uses these skills in my corporate career. I have done it and now you can, too, with my help.

Whenever you graduated, it defines you – it gives a hint as to your age to potential job interviewers and it also impacts your skills and talents that you can bring to your business and your career.

People who graduated more recently are more of "digital natives" than those of us who grew up with rotary phones really will ever be. That being said, those who are digital natives also still struggle with using computers for actual work purposes. We are all adept at using text speak (almost) but not necessarily able to craft the go-to cover or pitch letter to grow and define our careers and businesses. We will cover lessons on these items and more in this book.

We will use worksheets and interactive web site options to identify and move forward on your skills and your weaknesses – or what you can work on and how. I can even move it down to personalized learning plans, if you are willing to work with me to move forward.

For a refresher, here are some of the things I have recommended via my well-read blog on entrepreneur-ship and more

- Communication Skills:
    - Public speaking
    - Communicating through writing
    - Presentation Skills
- People skills
    - Managing
    - Teaching
    - Mentoring
- Networking

- o   Building relationships

- o   Identifying partnership opportunities

- Project Management

  - o   Time management

  - o   Matrix management

Where do you see yourself in each of these fields?

We will get into how to learn these skills in Chapter 3.

For Chapter 2, we want to focus on what you can do. What are you good at? Use this form to identify your strengths – let's just focus on strengths right now.

Strength:	Why:	How Long:

If you have more than 3 strengths; you are golden. A lot of people cannot identify their strengths or they get shy about it – this is not that time. You are an entrepreneur; your career is your business – or you are truly launching a business – you need to be cocky about what you can do but in order to highlight who you are. You want to make yourself indispensable on these traits.

What is it you are great at? How can you make that even greater? If you are still sitting here and telling me "nothing" I am going to tell you there are things you are great at and you should put them down and then commence to fake it until you make it.

At times, in our careers, as in life, we need to stretch to get to where we want to be with certain skill sets and more. Whenever I started a new job or switched careers, industries and more, I was also afraid of the things I did not know until I learned to just accept and embrace the things I did not know as learning challenges and highlight focus on the things I did know.

When I switched from the business side of project management to the technology side, even though I was clueless about "bricks" and "thick" vs "thin clients" – (I actually thought they were talking about someone's waist size) what got me through those meetings and more was the fact that I could analyze and add to any project by just jumping in and doing – while learning from those around me.

Can you access that quality? Did you hate learning as a child? I did, too. I was more focused in high school on my social life than school work; I was at best a "B" average through high school but when I got to college something snapped and I started studying and applying myself; I graduated with all A's, was class valedictorian and went on to receive a full tuition scholarship to the Rome, Italy campus right before I went out to give my speech.

You can fake it until you make it but you have to want to make it. Do not just plan on coasting by forever; you do need to meet those skill sets and apply them to your life to keep competitive and to keep being your own CEO.

What can you do that no one else can? How great are you at the things you are great at? I can tell you right now that if you can learn well, you can do anything. If learning is one of your skills, you are set for life.

Chapter 3:

What skills do you need?

What skills you need to be the boss of your own career or to launch a business includes working on new skills.

If these are not the skills you identified in chapter 2, these are what we need to work on to get your ready to rock out as the boss of your career or business.

These are some of the basic skills and I will be including my basic lesson on how you can be actionable on them and really improve your skill set.

- Communication Skills:
    - Conversational skills
    - Public speaking
    - Communicating through writing
    - Presentation Skills
- Project Management
    - Time management
    - Matrix management
- People skills
    - Managing

- Teaching
- Mentoring
- Networking
  - Building relationships
  - Identifying partnership opportunities

More On Skills

- Communication Skills:
  - Conversational skills
  - Public speaking & Presentation Skills
  - Communicating through writing

Communication Skills:

I am a huge proponent for communication skills; in fact I think you can stop reading the chapter after this part and still be heads above any of the competition out there. I am confident that when it comes to the top skill set needed for this day and age, it is communication skills. We all spend so much time attached to our smart phones, tablets, other communication devices that the rare person who is a good communicator is a sight to behold. For communication skills, these are the ideas behind improving and building out this group of skills that will help you be the boss of your business or your career.

Conversational skills

Some of the things you can do right now to help achieve better communication skills is to make a pact to keep your phone away; do not obsessively refresh your Facebook feed, do not rely on your phone to make you being somewhere alone "less awkward" by sitting with a device in your face, you are actually being more awkward, not less. Trust me. But everyone else is, too, so it seems ok. Instead, stay focused and in the moment, make eye contact and have conversations with others. Just by being in the moment as much as possible, you would be surprised at what you can accomplish.

You will set yourself apart from the rest; for instance, while waiting to be interviewed and if sitting with other applicants, keep your phone away. Make conversations, always be nice and present with the administrative folks at the company and make small talk. Does anyone remember what small talk was? It was what we did a lot more of before we had smart phones.

In this way, you can make potential allies, friends and networking partners.

Your homework:

Put the phone down and connect with individuals on your daily journey.

Public speaking & Presenting Skills

I am the prof who makes you present; this is not a joke or a test. You must have public speaking comfort levels to be the boss of your career or business. Anytime I am representing my company, I have to stand up in front of one or 20 or more people to discuss why I am the best person to be partnered with and / or to hire my company. As a corporate person, I was always highlighted and appreciated because of my speaking skills. It led to so many opportunities for me in corporate and it is the only way I can build and lead my business.

If I was uncomfortable speaking in public, I could not be an entrepreneur. I pitch my company everywhere and have documented how it was always easier for me to promote my company to strangers and how I struggled with discussing my company with people who know me in real life; this is something I had to get over quickly in my business planning and model. As I present my company to various partners, clients and more it is so important to be at ease, to remember my discussion points and to keep everyone engaged and focused.

Having this skill also helps in Corporate America, as I stated above so many of my opportunities were there because of my public speaking.

Here are some of my ideas on how you can become a more polished, professional speaker.

I would suggest you attempt to volunteer and speak at a class at your alma mater – this is a low risk option because any teacher would be happy to welcome you and make you feel at home and the students will only barely listen as best so this is a great practice arena. If you are not ready for this step, just think of how you act in meetings. Consider speaking up a few times in a small meeting session.

Maybe you do this already, then expand the size of your audience. Volunteer to give a presentation to management on something your department is working on. Build yourself up slowly, though. Do not jump in to volunteer to do anything client facing until you have done this enough time that you are ready to kick butt.

The 6 P's of Public Speaking

Prepare, prepare and prepare and practice, practice, practice – this is not a joke. You must know your content and ideas frontwards and backwards and be able to recite them in your sleep. You want to hit for dynamic speaker not just regular speaker although starting off as 'regular" speaker is great, too. I would like to see you though build into being dynamic, being able to engage the audience. Do this by faking it until you make it part of you.

As an undergrad, I traveled every weekend for the Speech and Debate Team and stood up in front of strange groups of 10 to 1000 and did prose, dramatic interpretation and more – every weekend for 4 years. I was terrible when I started and I built myself up to State and North East Regional Champion in Prose Competition for 1998 (seriously, my name is still in the books for both these competitions). I gave the valedictorian address at my college graduation in front of 1000's of people –

and when I did my MBA, I was the one who was always tapped to give the presentations and often walked away with the highest grade in the group so win/win.

I have been public speaking since 1994. The abilities I have, I was not born with. I mean, I am a Sagittarius so the idea is maybe that means I am more sociable and whatnot but I was not born giving speeches. It is a task and a lesson that I worked on, honed and get to the point where I am now comfortable speaking more at the drop of a hat and without much prep time.

You will not be here, yet. All that being said, I still get nervous before presenting or speaking. If I did not get nervous, I would think I was not human. Everyone gets nervous and what I have learned from being a professor for 13+ years and a presenter and more is that no one else knows you are nervous if you can hide it or otherwise focus your nervous energy.

How do you do this? Focus yourself by videotaping yourself giving a presentation and see what you do – do you shake? You might think you shake but is it noticeable? Does anyone see it? If yes, work on how to camouflage it or knowing you do it can help you stop doing it.

Do you have filler words like "uhm" "uh" or "like" – identify and consciously try to remove these filler words as much as possible. Do you touch your hair too much? Do you otherwise fidget? You will see these items in the video and be able to consciously try to correct for it. If you think you look so nervous in real life but when you watch the video you cannot tell you were nervous or show it to a friend and see if they notice anything – chances are high no one will be noticing the "nerves" that you think are so obvious.

Your Homework:

Create a video of yourself giving a talk about something important to you – watch it, critique it and send it to me via my Website as I want to see it!

Communicating through writing

This is another thing that takes practice, practice and more practice. Start writing something every day. Start writing for your imaginary audience. Who would you like to reach for your career or your business? What is the message you would like to share and to whom?

Craft these messages and identify how you need to write. Work on grammar, sentence structure – use less words than necessary, if possible. I have always been a wordy writer but in making blog posts and writing this EBook makes me work on my writing skills on a daily basis. The opportunities I have had as this company has been from the content I am creating and sharing – oh and I am using video and presentation / public speaking skills for that, too.

Your Homework:

Your homework is to write something – even if it is based off of another text - I did this exclusively when I launched my blog component of my site I only used other publications and wrote my opinions on that. Then I moved to creating my own content and I have never looked back. Write it and send it to me via my website – I want to read it!

We will discuss people skills and networking in future chapters and another installment will be on Project Management Skills.

Chapter 4:

Drafting the mission statement and YOUR plan

You know how when you go on an interview and you are asked, "Where do you see yourself in five years?" and you know how much we all hate that question – well, here is that question in triplicate for your work out for this chapter. Where do you see yourself in the short term (3-6 months), the medium term (1-2 years) and long term (3-5 years)?

Why is this important? You need to have a plan, a vision for your company and yourself. If you want to rock your career like a boss, you need to be managing yourself appropriately. What skills do you need to do X or Y? What degrees do you need? Who do you have to know? Who should you avoid? You need to have this on point and planned out oh and you need to revisit and change that plan accordingly as time goes by. For this reason, I am going to suggest you begin backwards. Start with your long term plans and work backwards so you can logically follow through in a timeline format on how to achieve these goals. You can have more than one plan. You need though to have at least one plan. Maybe you want to have two options one in career / corporate and the other as an entrepreneur. Be rational; do not assume you can get a PhD in two years if you have not even applied to the program yet. Make these goals aspirational but doable otherwise you will give up and never implement any of them.

Start with your mission statement or mantra. This should just be simply stating what makes you happy. Maybe you are happy being with your children; this is the key to unlocking your best path and your best self. You need to know what and where you are happiest and then build off of that.

For me, I knew once I had my children that I could not be traveling around the world anymore and that I wanted flexibility and more. My mantra was, in part, being with my children but then there is the other part of me that can only be fulfilled if I am using this brain and these capabilities I spent so long cultivating and learning.

I was able to build out on a long term goal the opportunity to be an educator, a professor and an entrepreneur. I am able to do all of this and unlock this potential because I followed my heart and what made me happy. This means I can (usually) be at pick up and drop off and any big school events, too. Also, I can help my kids with their homework while I am writing this book (yes, right now, as I type this, I am helping with homework).

Mission Statement:

FILL IN YOUR MISSION / MANTRA RIGHT HERE

_____

_____

_____

Notice I did not give you a lot of space for this; make it simple and straightforward with the potential to flesh it out in your plans.

Then think about your plans. I purposely put this backwards to make you envision your long term first, then your mid-term then you short term. This will show you logistically how the 3-planning cycles build out onto one another. Fill them out and take it with you at all times – you have a smart phone with a notes function or even use Pages to keep document with you at all times. Keep it and update it, as needed. Make your dreams real by keeping it on paper and reminding yourself of it at all times.

Long Term Plans

How do you achieve your mantra in the long term? How do you continue or achieve doing what makes you happy? For most of the world around us, people are unhappy. People can be unhappy because of deep sadness in their life (there are things that happen in this world, you should know if you even ever read a newspaper or watch the news that tragedy can be anywhere) and sometimes people are unhappy because they are just always that way – for some though happiness is something that can be achieved. If you know what truly makes you happy and not stress about anything else. Easier said than done but having these plans and working to accomplish them gives you a sense of agency /ownership and I truly believe will make you happier.

Do you want to be promoted? Do you want to have increasing responsibility – do you want to have staff reporting in to you? Do you want to be an executive? Where do you see yourself?

If you want to be an entrepreneur in the sense of business ownership, what do you think you want to launch? How can you build your business? Do you want your company to be launched? Do you have a company idea?

Identify your long term plan(s) – yes, not just one but multiple plans. See how many plans you can think of and plot out. Narrow all of it down to 3-5 long term plans. Maybe 3 are career related and 2 are small business ideas. The idea is that for everyone who works in corporate America, opportunities are dwindling, technology is making jobs obsolete and for some subsets of the population, entrepreneurship is the main push for opportunity (particularly immigrants and women of color are increasingly becoming entrepreneurial because of lack of opportunities in mainstream corporate routes).

I suggest that at least one of your backup plans be centered on entrepreneurial pursuits. This is the plan for the future and in the future if you do wind up with blank spaces on your resume (or you have some right now due to unemployment, caring for children, ill family members, etc), you need to have something to focus on and potentially build you up for these times of blank spaces.

It is my belief that to safeguard your career from these times of turbulence in jobs it is important to have a backup plan and maybe launching that side-gig while employed is a good way to help with the inevitable growing pains across a career.

YOUR HOMEWORK: - Your Long Term Plan

_____

_____

_____

_____

_____

_____

Medium Term Plans

This is your plan for 1-2 years out. You should have identified your two pronged plan starting here – one plan in corporate America and the other as your own boss. This is where the ideas start and begin to be built out. You need to consider what makes you happy and what you are good at. Everyone has the potential to do something on their own but sometimes it becomes in a time of desperation that people will consider it.

Identify your skills and what you want to be doing. Think about 1-2 years from now; where do you want to be?

YOUR HOMEWORK: - Your Mid-Term Plan

_____

_____

_____

_____

_____

_____

Short Term Plans

What do you want your career / business to focus on in the short term? When I began my career, I was all about finding a job. This was back in 1999 and I had an MBA and no real work experience.

I was a bit of a stand out in this respect. It was rare for people to go straight through for an MBA unless they were accounting majors but I left the country to do it so that was another layer of complexity on where I fit in once I came back to the US.

The one thing I know now that I did wrong was that I was looking for a job and not a career. This was a huge mistake – did you catch it right away? I should have been looking for a career and fast forward a few years after some near-disastrous mistakes, I was able to formulate a short term plan and execute on it to get on a career track.

Even as a business owner I need to have a short-term plan and when I re-launched this company in July 2015, I was focused on creating and sharing content and lessons and slowly but surely, I am doing that is so many ways and it has unlocked so many opportunities and now I need to focus more on my medium and long term plans, too. I do have them ready in my head, though.

So what can you do right now to make this plan? Think about where you want to be right now; do you want to stay at your current company? In your current industry? Do you think you will be staying where you are for long or do you want to branch out elsewhere?

Do you have an entrepreneurial plan in place? Is there something you can start to do right now on the side of your other jobs / responsibilities to launch this idea /plan?

This is your 3-6 month plan; what can you logically and possibly see happening / changing in 3-6 months? What little things can you do to push yourself on the road of the medium and long range goals you have?

YOUR HOMEWORK: - Your Short Term Plan

_____

_____

_____

_____

_____

Chapter 5:

Building Your Brand

You need to identify and build your brand as an employee and as a business. You can run your own life as if you are a business and you are the CEO.

Think about large companies and how they use social media and marketing to build out their brand. You are your own brand. You can identify yourself in this way and brand yourself for your next step or you can remain hidden in the shadows.

It is best to do this process slowly and to really rely on your common sense – even me as I build my brand and rely on myself to build it – my unique background as a professor/educator and executive, I still carefully consider everything I post and use common sense to try to avoid pitfalls and going "viral".

Yes, going "viral" could be a good thing but usually when it happens, it is not a good thing. I avoid topics such as politics and religion – this is a good rule of thumb for anyone – unless you are a politician or a religious leader, please try to avoid religion and politics as nothing can get as heated as those two topics.

That is really my number one rule is to think through everything you decide to on building your brand. Have a plan by answering these questions:

What do you want to build?

What do you want to be known for / as in your field?

Are you staying in your field?

Do you want to build yourself the option of being self-employed – as a free-lancer and/or a consultant or do you have another business idea?

How can you harness the power of social media and more to set yourself apart

You can use these techniques for both options and really you SHOULD be doing this for both options as today so much is found and identified online – many recruiters and hiring managers use LinkedIn before they even list an open job and you want to be in a position where people can find you and not where you are constantly trying to get people's attention.

Using social media and other methods to build your brand can be the best way to get this done and my lessons in this chapter will help you execute on this plan.

Start small:

Whatever it is you identify as your skills and or competitive advantage or subject you want to excel in, please start small.

Begin doing a lot of self-directed learning on the subject. What does this mean? Self-directed learning is learning you can do on your own with books, news items and even video learnings from trusted teachers (like me) or other options via YouTube. You can begin my using the tools and apps you use every day to compile learnings.

For Facebook, you can add in learnings and other news feeds to have the ability to learn while checking up on what your friends / frenemies are doing with their best lives shown on Facebook. This is a great way to start slowly with finding interesting news and other information to use to build out content knowledge and more to be able to eventually enter the conversation.

You can do the same thing with Twitter and Instagram. There are tons of industry niches and other content providers that are putting information and content through these services. You can begin your journey by learning. You should be learning every day.

This is how you can build out your success. I am a huge proponent and advocate for learning. If you follow me or read my content at all, you know that a big part of my "platform" or competitive standing is that everyone should continue to learn in the way that works best for them.

If reading and self-directed learning is not your thing, look into seminars, meetings, classes and / or industry events that you can attend and learn at in order to find your footing to begin your conversation about your brand. I am not saying you need to get layers of education and degrees in order to begin your conversation but you do need to be aware of more than just what you know to begin.

Since I have been an educator for 13 years, I am adept at weaving in many different content and learnings to make stories around knowledge and lessons – this is not something that I got good at overnight – I am constantly reading and learning as much as possible – definitely through teaching is how I get a lot of my learnings, too.

Identify your learning style preference –self-directed or learning with others – and find ways to get the knowledge started.

Once you feel that you know a little or even have something to say – so let's say you work in financial services and you have extensive ideas around how valuation works and you are at liberty to share this information – you can enter the conversation around this topic in baby steps first by maybe using Twitter or Facebook to share some articles about it with a little sentence or two about what you think about it. Then you can move out to using LinkedIn to add a statement or even a mini-blog post using LinkedIn Pulse about the topic.

Note: Please be sure you are at liberty to discuss what you are on the internet; do not give away proprietary information from your employer, do not trade on your employer's name and keep the topic open and something you can discuss without putting your career in jeopardy.

When in doubt, identify things that are your passion and that link up to your strengths and talents. If you are considering making a change to another industry, begin sharing and reading up on that industry. Then as you get more confident, branch out to joining some LinkedIn groups in the topic and adding some of your ideas there or opening up conversation on it.

If you have more content and are interested in building out more of a topic expertise, consider starting a blog.

How do you do that? My lessons involved many layers of web knowledge and background. I have been building Websites since 1999. The method and ease of building websites today is just out of this world compared to how it was in the past. I recommend and use Weebly; there are many options though and I will have more information in my Launch installment of this book.

No matter which you chose, just starting the site will not get you visitors, per se. Even using great SEO and other marketing techniques in the programming like Weebly allows for you to do quite easily, you still need to have more of a presence in social media to get your content out there.

You can do this by building off of your Twitter to begin compiling and sharing information in your expertise and then sharing your own content. I started using Twitter in late July 2015 and by January 2016, I had over 3000 followers and find a lot of traffic is brought to my site by my twitter activity.

I use SocialOomph to share and schedule tweets for my content. Twitter is like standing in the ferry terminal at a certain time and yelling something so when your tweet goes out depending on what you hashtag it for and what it says, at the time it goes out it can be noticed by ANYONE so if you send it out over and over, it has the ability to reach more people.

Plus, it is your content; you want people reading it and sharing it and using these services to schedule your tweets means you get the most eyeballs on your content; after all most people are not awake at 2am in their time zone to share content but at 2am in your time zone it is maybe 11pm or 8am somewhere else and having the tweets scheduled can mean other people who would normally not see it can see it.

Continue to identify and work on your writing style. Keep you writing as brisk as possible; try to find your conversational tone.

What is this? It is the writing style that is most like your way of presentation – if you do not have a presentation style, please consider practicing and learning more on how to be a good presenter. Make your content as clean as possible; use great grammar and punctuation rules.

Always keep it "clean" - sometimes a curse word will make your prose jump but consider your audience of potential hiring managers and /or business partners – is the risk worth it? Yes, it is a risk because not everyone sees profanity and jokes in the same light. Also, some jokes seem very funny to you internally but can be translated in lots of different ways. Just recently in my class, we were talking about Justine Sacco and how she used social media to tweet something so insensitive and infuriating but to her it was just a "joke". Due to that "joke" she was fired while in the air and did not even know about it until the plane landed.

Be very cautious with what you write and how your words can be read by the whole world – this is not the time to make an insensitive joke because it was funny at your fraternity / sorority meeting.

This is dangerous and troubling to do – content that you share and information that you write needs to pass the "test" the test used to be would you want to see it on the front page of the newspaper. Unfortunately, this rule of thumb is not as useful as it used to be as you can consider Facebook as a microcosm of a newspaper and people share just about everything on there and then some.

Everyone considers their social media on lock-down which maybe it can be but so much of what we put out there can potentially go viral and / or get shared by others without us being able to "control" the audience anymore. So many people make this misstep and it proves fatal for their careers.

I have been on Facebook since 2007-ish with a personal account but have always looked at it with side eye and been mercurial with what I share and how.

Now that I have relaunched my business I spend a lot of time creating, sharing and building content and I use social media exclusively to share my business, my capabilities and to build my brand. I could have been doing this for years building out my professional brand as an employee but I never did.

I have kind of fallen into this late in life or "Late" in life considering how others are now born on Facebook and using these sites to share their 'best life' to the public. It is interesting but at the same time it can be so difficult to deal with these sites and creating an online brand.

So many share personal photos, inappropriate jokes and more. You see the horror stories of the tweet that goes viral and gets someone fired or worse. I think we can all use some lessons.

My lessons is the place to be to figure out how to make social media work for you. I have found people are identifying and finding me through my posts and I hover before pressing publish on every post and read and re-read everything constantly to be sure I do not say anything inappropriate or otherwise make a mistake that will most definitely go viral.

So everything is a balancing act and there are times even still where I consider the risks and think about giving up and going back to "anonymity" – and I am not "famous" by any means – like I tell my mentees, you want to be the next guru not the next Kardashian.

I share and create content based on lessons, on learnings, and teachings and pulled from my 15 years' experience as an educator, executive and entrepreneur – what can you pull on to begin to create an online brand that represents YOU.

I can say that I get phone calls and messages and opportunities based on the information I share and people are seeing the value added in being involved or associated or hiring me and my business. If I had harnessed this power from the get-go, there is no telling where I would have wound up today. So do not make the same mistakes I have made – do not miss this opportunity. Thankfully I cannot speak to making the other mistakes of sharing the wrong things or sharing too much. Of course, you cannot control what other people do so it makes sense to Google yourself and make sure you are not exposed through other people.

Run your social media like an entrepreneur.

Consider the following tips:

Start small. Share some news articles pertaining to your career or field or where you want to be; also consider sharing your business idea or content in your potential business.

Have a social media set of accounts for your personal life and a different set for your professional life; also consider if you need another layer of personal career and personal side-gig level of media.

Build up after sharing information pertinent to your short medium and long term plans, think about branching out and creating some content.

Practice your writing skills using built in functionality of LinkedIn to comment on groups that pertain to what you want to be where you want to be.

Consider writing longer pieces through LinkedIn Pulse feature

Build out a website about you or a blog to share your thoughts and information

Once you begin sharing this type of information you will see you getting more followers and having the potential to build out more and more. Once you get to the point of creating and sharing content, you will be amazed at the opportunities that come up. I started with just one blog post; I am now at over 150 and that is content that is always being shared and gets new eyeballs and new interest in me and my brand that I am building in this way.

Chapter 6:

Writing Your Plan

It is important to continue to write and also to think about how to build out the appropriate documentation you need to run your business or to run your career like a business.

You need resumes, cover letters for your career and also pitch letters, proposals and more for your business.

For your career needs, the resume is really your one way to get your name out in front of people. But you can now also use LinkedIn to have a living breathing profile that shows who you are 24/7 and if you follow some of the tips in Chapter 5, you will get noticed but you need to have the best looking profile and the most current information available on your profile.

You do not want to attract attention for a potential job or interview through something you write on LinkedIn only to lose it because your profile looks terrible.

Remember LinkedIn is not Facebook it must be professional all the time. Your profile picture should just be a professional shot of you and as you want to be perceived; dress for the job you want not the one you have and please leave anyone else out of your profile picture – no family, friends, etc.

One quick professor tip is to take your resume and build it out so your LinkedIn profile matches and even exceeds the document. Since LinkedIn is technological by nature, you can include videos and / or other content and websites to make it pop.

Your resume should be the best document it possibly can. I have helped clients who paid big money from other providers and got fancy fonts, colors and designs but if the content sucks, no one cares about how it looks.

I tell the story of how I got into doing resumes over 15 years ago. When I was back from Italy in 1999, I was recommended to go see a "resume guru" who happened to be a lawyer but was a great resume editor. I was told that having a resume ripped up in red would be the best thing that could ever happen to a job seeker. I did not believe this. I thought my resume was perfect; I had just returned from Italy, I had an MBA, I was set.

The guru destroyed my resume and I remember it upset me because his manner was abrupt and he did not provide constructive criticism just ripped it apart – bear with me, I was 22 and not as skilled in people skills and understanding that not everyone does do constructive criticism.

This inspired me to take the lessons from him to start helping others with their resumes. I began doing friends and families and by 2003, I was doing all of my students resumes and more and more. I charged people sporadically but it was not my business plan at the time and in fact the business I launched in 2002-2004 was more centered on business consulting, PMP training and other ideas not on client management.

As a resume writer for the past 15+ years, the most important thing to do is to reflect the true you on this paper. You start off with the constraint of having just one page really resonate and represent you but it gets even harder when you can get to 2 or even 3 pages (dependent on years of experience really and /

or type of job search for instance in academia, a resume can be more than 3 pages etc.).

Your resume needs to truly shine – even as a business owner, resumes are important. The idea is that this paper is what should make you shine, should make people want to meet you and it can be fed into your LinkedIn profile.

The LinkedIn profile, though also needs more information and I would be remiss if I did not mention that I have constant content on my blog on resume writing and LinkedIn profiles and also that I have products for both items – a resume creation and also a LinkedIn profile 14-point proprietary improvement that you can find out more on my website about (www.thenextstep1234.com).

The cover letter also should be concise and specific to the position you are looking for – it can be generalized, if need be but really should be tailored to each request. Same for the pitch letter or the press release or the proposal about your business. Start small with your mission statement as discussed in previous chapters. Craft it, review it, share it and get feedback on it.

Resumes

More on resumes make sure the information you are most proud of is highlighted. Understand how to highlight the right information using the summary field – if you chose to use an objective or not to use an objective is a matter of preference. When I re-do resumes, I usually leave the objective out unless it makes sense to have it. The summary is where you can highlight some of the most important pieces of your background and experience but do not repeat it; these should be new sentences that do not repeat again in the body of the resume.

The work experience should be in chronological order and if there is a blank space in your timeline, use the summary to indicate what the reason was behind that blank space if you can do so comfortably and without sharing more than you want to share.

Keep in mind privacy and the right you have to it but also realize that if you posted things on social media like the recent Humans of New York post from someone who was in jail and said people do not know that they think he is in Hawaii, he kind of blew his cover on that.

There is a ton more advice and information on resumes for free on my blog www.thenextstep1234.com/blog under category Resume Advice.

Cover Letters

For cover letters, you must tailor each one to the job you are applying to as best as possible. Your information should pull from your resume without copying and pasting but with indicating your background and why you are a good fit for this potential role.

Please triple check your grammar, spelling and sentence structure. Make sure your letter is an interesting read but without being too interesting. You do not want to stand out for the wrong reasons like the countless cover letters that go viral for being too full of bragging and / or otherwise not professionally done.

Some samples of cover letters include the ones that are focused on industry or idea of position that can then be tailored further down to actual company / role.

Pitch Letter

This is more of a business orientated letter; something that includes your business elevator pitch and what you can do for the client, business or entity. There will be more on this in the next installment Entrepreneur-ing From Zero to Launch.

Press Release

A press release is a great way to share exciting news for your company. I have a template here:

The Next Step Announces College Readiness Seminar and EBook for High School Students (and Their Parents)

STATEN ISLAND, N.Y. — The Next Step, run by Lisa Vento Nielsen, is excited to announce a full college-readiness service that includes seminars, eBooks and one on one counseling for taking that step into education. Lisa Vento Nielsen has been an adjunct professor since 2003 and uses her unique experiences as an educator, executive and entrepreneur to motivate and inspire high school students while preparing them for their next step.

The offerings include a wide array of College & Career Readiness Seminars that have been launched at some local high schools. These seminars discuss topics from interviewing preparation to essay writing and includes life-skills such as managing stress and avoiding stereotypes. The focus is also on after college-graduation and building and managing successful career paths. These seminars are an interactive and engaging experience that highlights what it means to be from Staten Island and preparing for school while keeping an eye on the after-college career path.

There is also an EBook in production on College Readiness called: The Book on College Readiness: The Prof's Guide to Surviving High School and Kicking Butt in College & Career and for anyone interested in having a great read for both parents and student, the first chapter is available for free for anyone who signs up for it here http://www.thenextstep1234.com/new-ebook-college-readiness.html.

Bringing Ms. Vento Nielsen's teaching style, enthusiasm and years of experience to your high school aged student(s) is one of the smartest things you can do to prepare them for success.

The seminar and EBook give actionable lessons on preparing for the "real world". She also offers one-on-one application essay and resume creation for high school students at http://www.thenextstep1234.com/academic-essays-and-resumes.html.

The Next Step is locally owned business founded by Lisa Vento Nielsen, MBA, PMP. Ms. Vento Nielsen is a local Staten Island woman who attended St John Villa Academy and St John's University Staten Island and Rome, Italy campus for her BS in Marketing and MBA in International Finance, respectively. She is an educator, executive and entrepreneur who has been helping people identify and execute on their next steps in education and career for the past 15 years. You can find out more by visiting www.thenextstep1234.com or calling 347-733-9211. Follow The Next Step for daily blog posts on education, careers and more at www.thenextstep1234.com/blog or on Instagram and Twitter @thenext_step123.

Proposal

The proposal should discuss what you can do, how you can do it and more. Here is an example proposal template:

PORTFOLIO
[Subtitle]

About the Company

Products and Services

Blog Post Categories

Example Blog Post

Seminar Descriptions and Information

About the Company

The Next Step is a local company that is run by a woman who has over 12 years' experience as an educator, entrepreneur and expert in preparing for your next step.

Lisa Nielsen is a business executive, educator and entrepreneur. With her work in Corporate America, she has extensive hiring and resume experience. As an adjunct professor at local NYC colleges, her insight into what colleges want and how to present yourself is extremely valuable for your next step.

Lisa has a BS degree in Marketing and a MBA in International Finance, both from St John's University. Her MBA is from the Rome, Italy campus of St John's University, where she learned how to speak Italian. Upon returning to the United States, she began her career in the financial services and publishing industries. She excelled at Project Management and is a certified Project Management Professional since 2004 with PMI.

She left Corporate America to focus on teaching and entrepreneurial pursuits. Lisa began teaching at the University level in 2003 and learned she has a passion and a knack for teaching complex topics with a mix of real world and academic expertise.

Lisa has run her own businesses over the years as a consultant preparing business plans, editing and improving resumes and helping businesses, professionals and students take their next step.

Products & Services:

Resume Creation / Edit

Cover Letter Creation / Edit

Resume Creation / Cover Letter Package

Linked In Improvement

Academic Essay and Resume Package

Seminars, Trainings and Courses

Link to the Products:

http://thenextstep1234.weebly.com/store/c1/Featured_Products.html

Blog Post Categories

Her blog posts provide free information on improving your resume, interview tips and more. The links to some of my most popular blog categories are below:

- Resume Advice:

  http://thenextstep1234.weebly.com/blog/category/resume-advice

- Interviewing Tips:

  http://thenextstep1234.weebly.com/blog/category/interviewing-tips

- Managing Your Career:

  http://thenextstep1234.weebly.com/blog/category/managing-your-career

Blog Post Example:

A sample blog post that has been very popular (text) is here that I think ties in with what we were talking about today in terms of building a brand:

Prof Advice About Building Your New Brand

The first time I heard the term "brand" in reference to a person was back when I was in college, believe it or not. It sounded weird and bizarre and I could not wrap my head around how a person could be a brand - even as a Marketing major it made no sense. So for my second original blog post, I thought I would talk about how to build your own brand from my perspective - a marketing major/professor for whom it did not come intuitively.

I would say that even for my students and clients, the idea of being a brand is just not always an intuitive one. There are some people, though, who can run with the idea and successfully execute managing themselves as a brand from day one. I think that I am finally at that level of branding myself but it took me a long time, a lot of sweat and some major fears to overcome to execute on that plan. So here are my tips on how to build yourself as a brand.

Tip 1: Identify what you are great at

Know your sweet spot. What can you do better than most others? For me, this is teaching. I was always a teacher even when I did not know it - I used to tutor other kids in college on statistics and other subjects and when I did my MBA in Italy, I led some seminars on how to interview well and always had the most students vying to be in my groups - oh and led some late night Black Schole Model Training in the offices of the Rome Campus of St John's University (wow, la bella vita, huh?). Yes, I guess I am a nerd...

But I still did not realize or know how much teaching would become my passion. So how did it come about? I had a mentor (see Tip 2) who helped push me to be an adjunct - he was instrumental in me getting to Italy for my MBA and continued advising and helping me for many years after that. He encouraged me to keep applying to be an adjunct at St John's University even though each time I applied I was told that I was too young, too new out of Grad school and not the right fit. Until finally in 2003, I got the call. You see, an economics Prof had fallen and broken their neck (not fatally, thank God) but could not teach and as it was last minute, they needed someone, anyone and that person was me - what a way to begin my teaching career, right? At the time, I was working full time at Standard & Poor's but got special approval to work from home on Tuesdays and Thursdays so I could embark on being an adjunct professor. I taught a micro and a macro class to college freshman - could it be any more "boring"? But, I loved it and I was hooked and luckily was asked to come back to teach at nights in NYC campus and even a few super early classes on the Staten Island campus that fit into my work schedule.

Tip 2: Surround yourself with mentors and mentee others

It is important to have a team around you - people who can help you identify what you are great at and people that you can help do the same thing. This is a step deeper than networking - though networking should also be about what you can give and help other people with more so than what you will get back (because by giving, you will get back). This is having people who know you, people you rely on and trust their advice. This is a level of networking that is more focused on helping and creating long term relationships. My mentors have all been in my life between 5-18 years. But I also mentor others - and this is where I feel I truly learn and grow the most. Always work on building a team and giving back to others, too.

Tip 3: Do not be afraid to put yourself out there

I have said before that though I have been an entrepreneur since 2002, this is the first time I have taken my thoughts, my image and even videos of me and used them to communicate my thoughts and more around the business idea that I have to help people achieve their next steps. I have a vision in my head and heart for what this business is and how to execute it and this is the first time I allowed myself to be authentically out there and share that these thoughts and visions are mine. This has been the key to the success I am experiencing with this iteration of my business, in my opinion. It is because I was brave enough to write that first blog post, to send that first tweet and to be out there.

This is something you can do, too. Take something you know about, some business news you have a professional opinion on and write about it and/or use LinkedIn to share an update or to comment in a group. You can start with baby steps. You do not need to create a blog right away - but you should create a blog. Based off of Tip 1, you can create and share with the world that which is your passion. Just be careful about sharing professional opinions only and not personal opinions - that is when you can get into trouble. I would caution to avoid real hot topic issues like religion, politics, etc. Focus on building your brand out based on your skills and capabilities.

Tip 4: Never give up

I think this is important in terms of brand building for both entrepreneurs and corporate career path folks. If you do not get the promotion or the dream job you want, keep trying. Keep learning. Keep trying to espouse and represent the values you want to be known for - but make sure you followed Tip 1 so you know what those values and skills are you want to highlight.

What do you think of my quick 4 #proftips on how to build your brand? Do you think of yourself as a brand? Was it easy for you to think that way or not? Happy Hunting!

Seminars Information:

Seminar on How to Take the Next Step in Your Career led by Lisa Vento Nielsen, MBA, PMP

Professor Nielsen is an executive, educator and an entrepreneur who has spent the last decade helping professionals like you identify and execute on their life plans with the appropriate tools for success. Her business, The Next Step, is a well-known local provider of all things career orientated and her blog and social media are looked to for help in finding the next step for many people. Also, she is currently providing a certificate course to our adult learners on Entrepreneurship: Building Your Own Business.

She has designed this seminar program as a career planning boot camp to help anyone in any career who is interested in growing professionally or for those who might be in need of retooling and finding new employment. She also specializes in helping people who have been out of the workforce re-enter for such reasons as childcare or other unforeseen issues.

Her background in financial services and publishing industries and the over 15000 resumes she has reviewed all lend credence to the fact that she is a powerhouse in building your brand and achieving your next step.

This is meant to be a 3-part seminar workshop providing you with the tools and techniques you need to stand out from the crowd and achieve your next step in your career. You can choose to take just one of the seminars but it would be best for your career if you can take all three. If you take all three, you will get a discount.

Part 1: Resume/Cover Letter Intensive Workshop – Bring your resume and cover letter to work on improving it with a leader in resume editing and improvement. If you do not get enough call backs, you will improve your call backs after getting your resume improved and learning the tricks and tips on how to make your resume and cover letter stand out from the crowd.

Part 2: Using Social Media to build your Brand – Do you know how to use social media to represent yourself and stand out from the crowd? Using Twitter, LinkedIn and even a blog appropriately can put you head and shoulders ahead of anyone else –using them wrong can put you out of competition for any job. Learn what is the right and wrong way to use social media and how to network effectively OFFLINE as well as online.

Part 3: Interviewing Skills and Media Training – Are you prepared for any interview? What about being on video? Do you know how to use any medium to effectively communicate and get the job?

Please check out The Next Step and the blog to learn more about the type of information you will learn from Professor Nielsen – if you learn even one thing just be reading her posts, imagine how much you can learn in person over these action-packed seminars.

Seminars on Career Management – Embarking on Your Career in Project Management led by Lisa Vento Nielsen, MBA, PMP

The seminar is led by Professor Lisa Nielsen, MBA, PMP. She is an executive, educator and an entrepreneur who has spent the last decade teaching content and helping mentor and create project managers. Her business, The Next Step, is a well-known local provider of all things career orientated and her blog and social media are looked to for help in finding the next step for many people. Also, she is currently providing a certificate course to our adult learners on Entrepreneurship: Building Your Own Business.

Project Management is a new career path that you have already been doing, maybe without even knowing it. If you are new to your career path as a recent college graduate or are an older professional who is interested in branching out or re-tooling your skill set, these seminars are for you.

The seminar is broken up into 3 parts being offered in February 2016:

1) What is Project Management? What skills are included in Project Management?

   This seminar focuses on identifying PM skills you currently possess for use on your career path's next step
   This seminar is for those just starting their career paths as well as seasoned professionals either looking for a new challenge and/or hoping to differentiate themselves with a newly identified skill set.

   For recent grads, what did you major in? For any major (except accounting) there is not a job that says "Marketing major" or "Management Major" but there are lots of jobs that look for particular skillsets and abilities. Almost all work is project based with activities, teams that do not report to you and deadlines – identifying the Project Management skills you already possess and used as a student or employee can help give your resume the edge you need.

For those individuals who are more experienced, you have even more background and knowledge in Project Management than you currently realize. Learn how to gain the edge on your resume if you are out of work or currently employed – be prepared to grow your career with Project Management. This can be especially useful to people who have been out of the workforce and need to re-tool or re-train their skill set.

We will cover your experience and how to identify what Project Management is and what career paths there are for it. We will discuss career path identification what does it mean not learned in school or really on the job and being self-identified as a

2) Utilizing PM skills on your job search
How to use LinkedIn and other social media to highlight and move your job search forward as well as building your brand as a project manager. In addition, we will discuss treating your career path management as its

own Project for you to manage and execute your next step.

3) Planning and applying to take the PMP exam

I am an educator who has been teaching across genres, topics and grades and can make any content exciting and interesting. I will review the PMP process and give an overview of what the Project Management Institute is and the pieces you need to have in place to qualify for the exam. For those who qualify, we will be offering an exclusive 20-hour training course in preparing for the exam in April 2016. This designation is the equivalent for the CPA for the Project Management Industry. We will discuss the benefits of this certification and tips and techniques to prepare / apply for the exams.

Chapter 7:

On Networking, Mentoring and Building Relationships

This is where you identify and build out a relationship plan for your business and / or your career. I have my proprietary lessons for LinkedIn that I execute on for people who purchase my LinkedIn review but some of it will be told here in this chapter.

I share a lot of this on my blog and I do not want to repeat any content; this is all new stuff.

If you want to "entrepreneur-ing" your career, make sure everyone you know has a clear idea of your strengths and abilities and if you are looking to make sure that everyone knows you are looking and what you are looking to find. There is no shame in having people in your life know a little bit about you in a professional way. One of the best ways to do this is to identify and use social media as discussed in Chapter 5.

I remember for most of my career, my closest friends and even my husband really had no idea what I did in my career. It was complex, to a point, but I really never worked on applying these techniques of having a pitch that is understandable to all handy. I was able to speak to other technical and project management people but not able or I guess interested to convey that idea behind what I could do to others and this is where I definitely had a misstep.

Now, I spend a lot of time on missions and elevator pitches to really identify and share what I do to everyone. Being an entrepreneur means I should have been doing this for ever and with my corporate career but I did not – so lesson learned and a big reason as to why I write this book is to focus on the piece missing between being in corporate and being self-reliant on your growth and career path.

We all definitely can get complacent or even downplay our own abilities and achievements – I can tell you that as an entrepreneur if I do that, I will not have a business. There is a way to balance this ability and this focus of being entrepreneurial to your career and it is the only way to stand out in this crowded marketplace and to also be ready to go freelance, if needed.

By building your network, your relationships, being a mentor and a mentee, you can have the layers necessary to be ready to promote yourself, your business and others.

<u>Mentoring</u>

Be a mentor - by giving back to others and being in a great mentoring role, you can help yourself along the way. You can, by giving back and teaching someone else, be honing your skills on presenting, speaking and helping people be do-ers. This is a great skill for you to hone and to have. In having the ability to truly help another person in your field or in any field or maybe a younger person can lead to you improve your skills of teaching, motivating and more.

If you want to run your own business, having the ability to give back is major in terms of learning, doing soft-launches and seeing if there is demand for your skills and talents as an entrepreneur.

This also applies to your career; helps you to identify and share your skills. Finding people who are willing to mentor you is easier if you are also a mentor to others. It is in this way you truly identify the time commitment and the idea of the relationship. Your mentees are providing help to you and you can do this as a good mentee for others.

Be a mentee - You should also focus on finding mentors. Be a good mentee first and foremost. Do not be overpowering. Identify the relationships you would like to make, the help you would like always have questions to ask and be actionable on the answers; actually do what you ask information on and provide help back up to the mentor. See if there is anything you can help them with – as I talk about a lot as I help and mentor my students at times they give me feedback and help too on my website, social media and more.

Networking

This is as old as time. When I did this in 2000, it was just not done. I was an excellent networker. I sent out 60 letters to the people who were listed in the Beta Gamma Sigma directory who also went to my alma mater. My letter was straight and to the point highlighting what we had in common (both alums from St John's University and members of Beta Gamma Sigma) and indicating where I needed some help - I said I see you are working at XYZ firm from the handbook and I recently had jumped from Merrill to a dot-com and although I had a

MBA and some work experience that I felt lost and would love to meet with them to get their insight into what my next step should be and how I should take it. Of the 60 letters I sent out, I got over 50 meetings and some job offers and more from the exercise. Everyone said the same thing that they had never received such a letter before and that they would share my resume and contact information with their networks. It was an amazing feat and I stayed in touch with almost all of them for almost over a decade, give or take.

However, as time went on, I saw first-hand how they no longer could allow for other relationships to build like the ones I built with them – they became inundated with too many requests, constant requests.

What does this mean for now? It means that networking is not always about quantity but about quality. You want to identify and use your previous assignments for this book to help you do so – what are the things you want to learn, what the things you need to learn are. What industry do you want to be in? Whose career do you want to have? Start with your immediate friends, family and move from there into people in your current company, people in the company you want to work at, people who do what you hope to one day do – how can you identify and move forward with a few of these people to start to build your network.

Partnerships

This is more focused on when you run your own business – working in building partnerships, sharing content and perhaps making your income grow by leaps and bounds. Have an interesting story; share the story and have people aware of the story. If you are sharing your skills and abilities appropriately, you will perhaps find partners interested in building their businesses with you. It is up to you to select and agree to partnerships.

Always try to make sure the skills and culture of the organization aligns with what you want to do with your business and your brand. Do not partner with just anyone; make sure there is a synergy and the ability for both parties to grow.

I have a partnership with Wagner College Office for Lifelong Learning where I provide training, content, curriculum and more and they promote and share my content and courses, too. This partnership is a natural connection between what I do and what they offer to their clients and students. Identify and try to find partnerships like this but if you follow my social media plan and consider checking out my new EBook on How to Blog Like a Pro – fessor for more execution tips but if you do these things to build and brand yourself as an expert, you can find yourself being searched for in terms of partnership agreements and more.

One thing I have noticed as an entrepreneur and a sole proprietor is that you do have to watch how many irons you have in the fire to prepare for the great revenue streams and being a project manager by trade means I know how much time things can take and how to budget my time to match my deliverables.

Chapter 8:

MANAGING SUCCESS & REACHING BACK

This is so important – to not only build your business but to consider giving back and offering services at a discount or for free for those who need them. Really think about who you are and what you would like to do to give back and then try to do it.

I know how hard it can be to schedule and to make time where you are not making money as an entrepreneur, it is hard to do but my belief is that by doing this, it gets your name out there, it also provides good feelings about you and your business and this can never be a bad thing. However, I do caution that you not take on too much at once.

You do need to handle your deliverables and your client needs first and then with the left over time focus on carving out a little bit to give back. Maybe you would like to provide some free advice to your high school or you want to volunteer somewhere with your unique talents and abilities. Identify what it is you would like to do.

My story is an interesting one because what started as a give-back has become a product line and I think you can find this happening for other small business owners, too. There is two layers to giving back – one where you know it will not potentially lead to income and another that might lead to income.

I do both; for the one that could potentially have led to income, it is going down that path as I write this. Back in 2012, I envisioned doing a college readiness seminar but at the time I had a 2 year old and a 5 year old and that was just not happening. However, I kept thinking about it and when I relaunched this company in July 2015, it became something I began working on immediately but it was organic - I already had the background I needed to create and share the content. I started slowly but also focused on other things and before I knew it I was ready to do it for free for some local schools and then found there is a paying method for this information and background that I bring to the table I just needed to expand on my content and get out there more and more.

For other events, in my community outreach, I select one or two charities where I can do the most good – where I can roll my sleeves up and work on resumes, application essays and even provide tutoring for GED exams and more.

What can you bring to the table for volunteering and how can you balance it for the type that will pay you back in good feelings and the kind that could potentially pay you back in a new career. The more I build out my business and apply my entrepreneur-ing tricks and skills to my career, the more opportunities that are opening up and becoming available to me and my business and I want to see the same for you in your career and / or your business.

I want to encourage you to consider doing something on the side; if time and brain power are available – do not ever stop learning – continue to apply learnings and lessons from this book, my blog or my seminars and trainings that I offer in the NYC area to keep yourself sharp and open to any opportunity that comes your way. Run yourself like a Fortune 500 company but leaner, more agile and better – put investments into yourself with classes, learning and more to keep yourself focused on being the best you that you can be. The only way to do this is to continue to learn every day and to make yourself competitive in the crowded marketplace. I will repeat again because it is so important that you must have speaking skills and presentation skills – really consider giving back in a capacity that forces you to dust off these skills, increase these skills and to make yourself a "teacher" in any way you can – this will be what makes your career or business stand out and can help you in all matters of your life.

Chapter 9:

Execution and Feedback Loop

This is where I state again that you can institute a feedback loop using my contact information to be in touch every step of the way as you build out your strategy for entrepreneur-ing your career or your business (or both).

Once you complete your mission and your plans, send them over to me; use social media to share with me to discuss with me and / or to get a free one on one consultation with me.

If my templates are helpful or you would like to suggest changes, edits or additions to this EBook, I would like to hear that, too.

Consider me your personal Professor on how to use Entrepreneur-Ing to build your career or your business.

Thank you for reading me EBook and continue to follow me on Social Media – Twitter & Instagram @thenext_step123 and Facebook at https://www.facebook.com/TheNextStepLisa/ and my blog www.thenextstep1234.com/blog.

More EBooks are in progress on:

Going from 0toLaunch – Everything you need to know to be an entrepreneur as of today

College and Career Readiness

How to Blog Like a Pro-Fessor

Thank you to all who read this book and please reach out and let me know how you are applying these Entrepreneur-ing principles to your life, your career and your business. Happy Hunting!

What is The Next Step?

The Next Step is built around college and career readiness. My experience as an educator and an executive helps new graduates, high school students and career professionals take their next steps to career and education goals.

I create content and offer interactive and informative seminars on college and career readiness, entrepreneurship, and more.

Also, I work one-on-one with clients to help them with resumes, cover letters, LinkedIn profiles and application essays. As part of my service, I include coaching and career plans without extra cost.

I am interested in speaking at your event to teach how to be ready for the next step.

Lisa Vento Nielsen, more at
www.thenextstep1234.com